ALFONSINA STORNI
SELECTED POEMS

Edited by Marion Freeman

Translated by Marion Freeman, Mary Crow,
Jim Normington, and Kay Short

WHITE PINE PRESS

Some of these translations have previously appeared in: *The Webster Review, Anthology of Magazine Verse, Contemporary Women Authors of Latin America, The Minnesota Review,* and *Compages.*

ISBN 978-0-934834-16-2

Designed by Watershed Design

Cover design by John Sorbie

Publication of this book was made possible, in part, by grants from the National Endowment for the Arts and the New York State Council on the Arts.

WHITE PINE PRESS
76 Center Street
Fredonia, New York 14063

CONTENTS

ALFONSINA STORNI
SELECTED POEMS

ALFONSINA STORNI: AN INTRODUCTION

Alfonsina Storni's biographers tell us that Argentines hailed her as a "national glory" during her lifetime. The epithet is no doubt due in part to her unique poems about the city of Buenos Aires and its river Plate. It is therefore surprising to learn that this "Argentine" poet was born, not in Argentina, but in Switzerland. Her Swiss parents, who had emigrated to Argentina in 1885, returned to Switzerland in 1889 for an extended visit. Their third child, Alfonsina, was born in the village of Sala Capriasca in the Italian Swiss Canton of Ticino on May 29,1892.

Storni's early years were difficult. Almost immediately after the family returned to the Argentine city of San Juan, their fortunes began to decline, although earlier they had been leaders of the business and social life there. Storni's father Alfonso, began to drink, neglected his business, and was absent for long periods of time. When the family moved to Rosario after the father's death in 1906, it was the poet's mother, Paulina, who struggled to support her family by establishing a school and taking in sewing. Storni's formal education was haphazard and she later commented that her childhood generally lacked supervision and direction. However, as early as her thirteenth year she began to work in a hat factory to supplement the family income, and the next year her dramatic ability earned her a place in a theatrical company which hired her as it passed through Rosario and with which she toured for a year. In the poem "Women Pass By," from her book *Languidez*, she says of her early life:

> My poor mother says that, as she saw things,
> I learned very early the science of tears.

Commentators on Storni's poetry have pointed to a special ability to create dramatic situations and a conversational tone which are unique features of her verse, as well as her later fame for public readings of her own poems, but her year on the road also taught her that she needed a more stable existence. Therefore, in 1909 she enrolled in a school for rural teachers. The course lasted two years, and Storni worked at the school as well as secretly in the chorus of a theater of questionable reputation in order to pay for her studies. When her work in the chorus was discovered, it created a minor scandal which in turn prompted Storni to leave a suicide note and run away. But the incident quickly blew over; suicide was not a serious alternative at this moment in the poet's life.

In 1912 Storni found herself in Buenos Aires with her diploma and an infant son. It was a daring move, but she felt the need to flee provincial gossip for the relative anonymity of the capital. Her first years in Buenos Aires, without friends or work, were times of great personal and economic hardship. She found employment working as a cashier, and eventually won, over a large pool of male applicants, a decent-paying position in an import firm. The work was not satisfying, but she was grateful for it and took her duties seriously. Her first poems appeared singly in magazines, and in 1916 Storni published her first volume of poetry, *La inquietud del rosal (The Restlessness of the Rosebush)*. The poems showed a strong influence of the waning *modernista* movement, roughly equivalent to European symbolist poetry, and while reviewers were harsh in their criticism, they saw promise of better poetry to come. The poet herself later deplored this early work and attempted to exclude it from a volume of her complete works published shortly before her death, but she admitted that she wrote it "in order not to die." In several poems of this first volume, the poet who is still feeling her way toward her own mode of expression states that she wishes to speak in a voice that is uniquely hers. For example, in the poem, "La loba" ("The She-Wolf"), she says:

> I am like the she-wolf.
> I broke from the pack
> And, tired of the plains,
> I went to the hills.

In the years immediately following the publication of her first volume, Storni became an integral member of the "penas" or groups of intellectuals of Buenos Aires whose members read or performed their own and others' works, discussed topics of current interest, and arranged cultural events. She was the first woman accepted into the Buenos Aires intellectual community, and thus more often than not was the only female present at their gatherings. It was among these friends and colleagues that she began to achieve renown for her dramatic reading of her own poems. As a result, Storni's friends created two posts for her, a special position in the Lavarden Children's Theater and a chair of reading at the Normal School of Modern Languages. These and other teaching positions enabled her finally to work as an educator, the profession for which she was trained and to which she wholeheartedly devoted her energies, often to the point of physical and mental exhaustion. Also during these early years in the capital she published three more volumes of poems: *El dulce dano (The Sweet Pain)* in 1918; *Irremediablemente (Irremediably)* in 1919; and *Languidez (Languor)*, in 1920.

In these volumes Storni continues to develop the themes from her first work—nature, especially the springtime, the desire to dance, the sea in relation to death, and love, principally from the woman's point of view—themes which she will continue to develop and rework throughout her life. These books were immediately popular and are still her works which are most widely read and for which she is best known. The poems of these three volumes often reflect the expectation of youth, especially in love. Many poems voice highly personal pleas for a satisfying relation with a man who will see and accept her for what and who she is. In spite of her solitary but successful struggle for survival in a world of harsh reality, Storni seems to say that woman is incomplete without a partner, yet she more often than not ends by acknowledging the impossibility of the ideal of love for which she cries out. Well known poems from this group which express her disillusionment with men include "Tu me quieres blanca" ("You Want Me White") in which she rejects the double standard and exhorts men to be pure if they expect the same of her, and the poem, "Hombre pequenito" ("Little Man"), which ends with the admission of a lack of understanding on the part of both sexes. Complaining that the man who has encaged her will never understand her, she admits:

> Neither do I understand you, but meanwhile
> Open the cage for I want to escape.
> Little man, I loved you half an hour,
> Ask no more of me.

Poems such as these have led to her reputation as a feminist, and others in these volumes reinforce this view of her. For example, in "Bien pudiera ser" ("It May Well Be") she speaks of her mother's frustrated dreams of liberation from being one more "silent woman" of her repressed family, and states the belief that she herself has finally broken that tradition. In these poems Storni clearly recognizes herself and her writing as breaking new ground.

Five years pass before the 1925 publication of *Ocre (Ocher)*, the volume which Storni considered her best. It is a work of transition, containing much from her earlier poetry but also striking out in new directions. Thus while the love theme is present, the poet looks on it with less involvement. Regarding form, Storni continues to prefer the sonnet, as before, but begins to experiment with rhyme and verse form, and shows a new economy of language. And although she further develops "female" themes such as woman's being determined by outside influences such as moon phases and the nature of her body, she now speaks for all womankind rather than for herself alone. As the autumn color in the title indicates, in *Ocher* the older Storni begins to view the world with a maturity and an understanding absent in her earlier works.

New directions in form, and to a lesser extent in content, characterize Storni's last two volumes. *El mundo de siete pozos (The World of Seven Wells)*, published in 1934, marks the end of a hiatus of nine years in her poetic output, and *Mascarilla y trebol (Mask and Clover)* appears shortly after her death in 1938. In the first of these books she abandons formal structure for a free verse with emphasis on rhythm and with thematic, rather than structural, unity, while all the poems in *Mask and Clover* are a return to a more structured form in what the poet called "antisonnets," that is, poems composed with the traditonal two quatrains and two tercets of the classic sonnet but without rhyme. Although most of her earlier themes persist in reworked form in these last books, new and original themes appear alongside them. Most notable are her poems about the city and its dehumanizing effect on the individual spirit, and, long before the appearance of Neruda's odes, poems dedicated to ordinary objects such as a hen, a tooth, a pencil. An example of new attitudes toward old themes is the antisonnet "A Eros" ("To Eros"): the poet finds the doll Eros on the beach, opens it to discover its inner workings, which include a trapdoor labeled "sex," and then tosses it all into the sea.

These last two works are the fullfillment of that promise made by the "she-wolf" to break from the pack and speak in her own strong voice. The world of seven wells, or openings, is the human head and senses. In these volumes Storni sets about to apprehend the world through her senses and her intelligence. Where earlier nature and other realities could only be expressed subjectively, as they related to the poet's emotions, now she approaches the world from new angles— fantasy, the surreal, irony, or wonder. Storni is never totally absent from her poems, but there is a new distance between her and the reality she views, a detachment that often borders on the cynical, as in the case of her treatment of the god of love in the poem "To Eros."

Early reviewers of Storni's last two volumes accused her of losing her lyricism and writing obscure verse. The poet herself was aware that these would not be popular works, and asked the reader's cooperation and use of the imagination. However, more recent opinion views these works as her true beginnings as a human, and not just feminine, poet. Her previous work, never intellectual but frequently cerebral in its honest questioning of accepted values and her role in the scheme of things, foreshadow her final volumes in which the poet has come to terms with her reality and found a way to express it in her own unique voice. In spite of her undeniable feminism, they earn her a place beside the major Spanish American poets of both sexes.

In 1935 Storni discovered that she had breast cancer. Although she underwent surgery, the malignancy returned. Unwilling to go under the surgeon's knife a second time, in October of 1938 she left Buenos Aires for a favorite oceanside resort, wrote a final poem, "Voy a dormir" ("I Am Going to Sleep"), and ended her life in the sea. In the poem, she calls to her "fine nurse," who has teeth of flowers, hands of herbs, and wears a cap of dew, to prepare the earthen bed of springtime in which she will gladly sleep. October is her favorite month, the beginning of the Argentine spring, and the manner of her death makes her frequent association of death and the sea in her poetry a prediction of her own life's end.

If Storni's last book opens with the poem "To Eros," in which the poet has uncovered love's deceit, it significantly ends with "A madona poesia" ("To My Lady of Poetry") where Storni, kneeling at the foot of her saint, declares her faith in and dedication to the demands of the art for which poetry branded her with its "fierce iron." A woman who lived an unconventional life for her time, a life that was, as a result, often fraught with conflict and struggle, Storni was aware that in her poetry she likewise broke through the traditional boundaries of what had previously been considered appropriate for women. During her lifetime, she suffered for that, too, but her farewell poem in her final volume of poetry seems to say that her poetry was her most precious possession and, in the end, the justification for her life.

—Marion Freeman
—Colorado State University

ALFONSINA STORNI
SELECTED POEMS

THE SHE-WOLF

I am like the she-wolf.
I broke with the pack
And fled to the mountains
Tired of the plain.

I have a son, the outcome of love without marriage,
For I couldn't be like the others, another ox
With its neck in a yoke; I hold my proud head high!
I plow through underbrush with my own hands.

Look how they laugh and point at me
Because I've said "The little sheep bleat
When the she-wolf enters the corral
Because they know the she-wolf came out of the wilds."

Poor little tame sheep in a flock!
Don't fear the she-wolf, she will not harm you.
But also don't belittle her, her teeth are sharp
And in the forest she learned to be sly.

The she-wolf will not steal your shepherd, do not fear;
I know you were warned and that you are afraid,
But without reason, for the she-wolf
Doesn't know how to steal; her teeth are weapons of death.

She entered the corral out of desire
To see why the flock was frightened
And how they hide their fear behind laughter
their every gesture betraying a strange sorrow...

Go see if maybe you can face the she-wolf
And steal her cub but don't go with the flock
Or follow a shepherd...
Go alone! Oppose her courage with power and strength!

Little sheep, show me your teeth. How tiny they are!
You poor little ones can't go anywhere without your masters
Through the rugged mountains, because if a tiger waits for you
You're defenseless and will die in the wilds.

I am like the she-wolf. I travel alone and I laugh
At the flock. I exist on my wages and they're mine
Wherever I decide to go, for I have hands
That know what work is and my mind is sound.

She who can follow me can come along.
But I am on foot, facing the enemy,
And I don't fear life or its fatal rage
Because I have in my hand a knife which is always ready.

My son comes first, then me and then whatever happens.
Destiny may call me quickly to the struggle.
Sometimes there's the illusion of the bud of love
Which I know how to stifle before it flowers.

I am like the she-wolf.
I broke with the pack
And fled to the mountains
Tired of the plain.

JN

SQUARES AND ANGLES

Houses in a row, houses in a row,
houses in a row.
Square, square, square
houses in a row.
People now have square souls,
ideas in a row
and angles on their backs.
I myself shed a tear yesterday,
my God, it was square.

MC and MF

WATER

Water, water, water!
I go shouting through streets and plazas
water, water, water!

I don't want to drink it,
I don't want to gulp it.

It's not my mouth that asks for water;
my soul's drying out,
it itches from dryness.

That's why I go out through streets and plazas
begging (so urgently):
water, water, water!

Open my veins,
pour into them the clear current of a river.
Water, water, water!

MF

YOU WANT ME WHITE

You'd like me to be white as dawn,
You'd like me to be made of foam,
You wish I were mother of pearl,
A lily
Chaste above all others.
Of delicate perfume.
A closed bud.

Not one ray of the moon
Should have filtered me,
Not one daisy
Should have called me sister.
You want me to be snowy,
You want me to be white,
You want me to be like dawn.

You who have held all the wineglasses
In your hand,
Your lips stained purple
With fruit and honey
You who in the banquet
Crowned with young vines
Made toasts with your flesh to Bacchus.
You who in the gardens
Black with Deceit
Dressed in red
Ran to your Ruin.

You who keep your skeleton
Well preserved, intact,
I don't know yet
Through what miracles
You want to make me white
(God forgive you),
You want to make me chaste
(God forgive you),
You want to make me like dawn!

Run away to the woods;
Go to the mountain;
Wash your mouth;
Get to know the wet earth
With your hands;
Feed your body
With bitter roots;
Drink from the rocks;
Sleep on the white frost;
Renew your tissue
With the salt of rocks and water;
Talk to the birds
And get up at dawn.
And when your flesh
Has returned to you,
And when you have put
Your soul back into it,
Your soul which was left entangled
In all the bedrooms,
Then, my good man,
Ask me to be white,
Ask me to be snowy,
Ask me to be chaste.

MF and MC

JOURNEY

Tonight I look at the moon
white and enormous.

It's the same as last night
the same as tomorrow.

But it's foreign, because never
was it so huge and so pale.

I tremble like
lights tremble on water.

I tremble like
tears tremble in my eyes.

I tremble like
the soul trembles in the body.

Oh the moon has opened
two silver lips

Oh how the moon has spoken to me
these three ancient words:

'Death, love, and mystery...'
Oh my flesh is nearing its end.

Above the dead flesh
my soul becomes confused.

My soul—a nocturnal cat—
rises up over the moon.

It travels through the enormous sky
crouched low and sad.

It travels through the enormous sky
up over the white moon.

JN

LITTLE-BITTY MAN

Little bitty man, little bitty man,
let your canary loose that wants to fly away.
I'm that canary, little bitty man,
let me go free.

I was in your cage, little bitty man,
little bitty man who gives me a cage.
I say little bitty because you don't understand me
and never will.

Nor do I understand you, but meanwhile
open up the cage, for I want to be free.
Little bitty man, I loved you half an hour.
Ask no more of me.

MC and MF

OLD MOON

Your winter arms protect me.
Under your tender care
I let the hours pass in lethargy
Sad and long.

I feel everything dear to me,
Clarity walks beside me.
I even love the evil that wounds:
Pity anyone dying!

Oh, old moon, fleshless world,
Wandering through the skies in deep silence.
How much warmth my lover has...
Moon, aren't you cold?

MF

IT COULD WELL BE

It could well be that all I have felt
was only whatever was never meant to be,
was only something forbidden and repressed
from family to family, from woman to woman.

They say that in my people's ancestral homes
what we should do has been meted out.
They say that women have been silent
in my maternal home... Oh, it could well be...

At times my mother was attacked by the whim
of liberating herself, but before her eyes
a deep bitterness rose up, and she cried in the shadows.

And all of that, biting, conquered, mutilated,
all that she found shut up in her heart—
without wanting to, I think I've liberated it.

MF

ANCESTRAL WEIGHT

You said to me: My father didn't cry;
You said to me: My grandfather didn't cry;
The men of my race have never cried,
They were men of steel.

While you were speaking, a tear sprouted on your cheek
And fell into my mouth...I have never drunk
So much venom from so small a glass.

Weak woman that I am, poor woman,
Woman who understands,
I knew the pain of centuries when I tasted it;
This soul of mine cannot stand up
Under all that weight.

MC and MF

THE CLAMOR

Once, when I was passing life by,
Out of pity, out of love,
Like a fountain that gives everything,
I gave my heart.
And I spoke to the others who were passing by
Without malice, maybe with fervor:
"I obey a law which governs all of us:
I've given my heart."

And as soon as I had spoken, like an echo,
The voice came back to me:
"Look at the bad woman, that one passing by:
She's given her heart."

From mouth to mouth, over the rooftops
This cry went rolling:
"Throw stones at her, yes, right in her face!
She's given her heart."

Now it's red with blood, yes, my own face,
But not from shame
For I turn face to face to the men and I repeat:
"I have given my heart!"

MC and MF

SHE WHO UNDERSTANDS

Her black hair falling forward,
The beautiful woman, middle-aged,
Kneels, and a suffering Christ
Looks at her with pity out of his hard wood.

In her eyes the weight of an enormous sadness,
In her breast the weight of a child to be born,
At the foot of the bleeding white Christ she prays:
"Lord, this child of mine, don't let it be born woman!"

MF

THE MERCY OF THE CYPRESS

Traveler: this cypress which rises
a mile from your feet and in whose top
a little bird sings his love
has a delicate soul beneath its rough clothes.

It rises so high from the ground
to give you an immaculate vision,
for if your glance searches for its top
you will stumble, human, onto heaven.

MF

COLDNESS

A harsh cold unleashed its news
and harassed people, stumbling,
like rats, through the city
looking for their caves.

Lined up in the streets,
necks and hands hidden in cloth,
muffled in coats and furs,
they look like bundles.

But farther away, my vision never saw
such a clean moon and sky.
While people shiver, that sky is a
beautiful irony.

Almost as if a voice that descended
from the disdainful clean blue
mocked their discomfort saying to them,
"Now listen to me!"

MF

THEY'VE COME

Today my mother and my sisters
came to see me.

I'd been alone a long time
with my verses, my pride...almost nothing.

My sister,the oldest one, has grown up,
she's a blond; her first dreams are passing
before her eyes. I said to the youngest one:
"Life is sweet. It all ends badly."

My mother smiled as people
who know souls well usually smile;
She put both her hands on my shoulders,
looked hard and long at me
and I suddenly began to sob.

We ate together in the warmest room
in the house.
A springtime sky...
All the windows were open so we could see it.

And while we calmly talked
of so many old, forgotten things,
my sister, the youngest, interrupted:
"The swallows are passing..."

MF

13

THE THORN

I was wandering aimlessly,
without seeing the harsh broomplant
exploring with its branches
the pleasant path.

An emerald arm
armed with long spikes
nailed a thorn into my skirt
and held me at its side.

And one day
when I was wandering idly
your eyes stopped my step
like a wild thorn.

The difference: I managed to rid myself
of the buried thorn,
but when can I get free
of your harsh look?

MF

TWENTIETH CENTURY

I am being consumed by life,
Wasting, not doing anything,
Between the four symmetrical
Walls of my house.

Oh, workers! Bring your picks!
Let my walls and roof fall,
Let air move my blood,
Let sun burn my shoulders.

I am a twentieth century woman.
I spend my day lounging,
Watching, from my room,
How a branch moves.

Europe is burning,
And I'm watching its flames
With the same indifference
With which I contemplate that branch.

You, passer-by, don't look me
Up and down; my soul
Shouts its crime aloud, yours
Hides its under words.

MF

DELETED

The day I die the news will follow
Its practical course
And immediately from office to office
In official record books they'll look for me.

Somewhere far away in a little town
Which sleeps in the mountain sun
In an old record book
A hand unknown to me
Will draw a line through my name.

JN

LITANY FOR A DEAD EARTH
(for Gabriela Mistral)

There will come a day when the human race
Will have dried up like a dead vine,

And the ancient sun will be
Like the useless ashes of a burned torch.

There will come a day on the frozen earth
When there will be a sad and total silence:

A huge shadow will encircle the earth
And spring will never return;

The dead earth, like a blind eye,
Will go on turning without peace forever

But in the darknesss, all alone, groping
Without a song or a moan or a prayer.

All alone, with her favorite creatures
Exhausted and sleeping in her womb.

(Like a mother who goes on even though she has
the poison of dead children in her womb).

No city will be standing... the earth will support
Ruins and rubbish on her dead shoulders.

From a distance black mountains
Will look on without caring.

Maybe the sea will be nothing more
than a block of ice, dark like all the rest.

And then, anguished and motionless,
It will dream of ships and waves,

And pass the years trying to ambush
Any boat that plows through its breast.

Where the sea meets the earth
It will create illusions on the beach with the moon,

It will try to make
the moon another mausoleum.

Uselessly the block of ice will want to open its mouths
To swallow rocks and men,

To hear the horrible screams
Of shipwrecked sailors wailing endlessly:

Nothing will remain; from pole to pole
A single wind will have swept it all away:

The seductive palaces of Spain
And the miserable huts of Bedouins;

the hidden caves of Eskimos
And lavish delicate cathedrals.

Blacks, yellows, browns,
Whites, malays, mestizos...

They will meet beneath the earth
begging each other's pardon for so much war.

Holding hands they will surround
the entire earth in a circle.

And they will moan in a sad chorus:
"O what useless, stupid suffering!

The earth was a garden full of roses
And excellent cities;

Some were built along rivers
Others around forests and lakes.

Delicate rails stretched between them
Like threads of hope;

The fields bloomed and everything
Was pleasing and fresh as a meadow;

Yet instead of understanding, we stood
Brother against brother, knives in our hands;

Women slandered each other
and merchants colonized the earth;

We all fought against the good
And covered it with mud and poison...

And now we are white bones
Surrounding the earth in fraternal patrol.

Now there is nothing left
Of the brief flash of humanity."

* * *

Could be some mute statue
might remain, alone and naked.

Plowed by the shadows it might be
The last refuge of humanity.

The last refuge of that form
Made in God's image,

That form in which God, overcome by its subtlety,
Found beauty without knowing it.

Perhaps some gentle star
Will ask: "Who is she?

Who is this statue of a woman who dares
To move by herself through a dead world?"

And it will love her by celestial instinct
Until she falls at last from her pedestal.

Perhaps one day, because of some nameless mercy,
The light of a wandering sun

Will rekindle in its fire
this poor earth and its people.

And will timidly suggest to it: O tired earth
Dream for a moment of spring!

Absorb me for an instant: I am
the universal soul which changes and never rests...

How they will move beneath the earth,
Those dead who are closed inside her womb!

How they will push toward divine light
wanting to fly toward what enlightens them!

Those dead eyes will try in vain
To reach the red rays.

In vain! In vain! The mud piled
Over their bones will be too thick...

Defeated and stacked together
they will not be able to leave their ancient nests,

And to the call of a passing star
No one will be able to cry: I love!

JN

WORDS TO MY MOTHER

I don't ask you to tell me the great truths
Because you wouldn't tell me; I only ask
If, when you carried me in your belly, strolling through
Dark patios in bloom, the moon was a witness.

And if, when I slept listening
In your breast with its Latin passions,
A hoarse and singing sea lulled you to sleep nights
And if you watched in the gold dusk, the sea birds plunge.

For my soul is all fantasy, a voyager,
And it is wrapped in a cloud of dancing folly
When the new moon ascends the dark blue sky.

And, lulled by a clear song of sailors, it likes—
If the sea unlocks its strong perfumes—
To watch the great birds that pass without destination.

MF and MC

FORGETFULNESS

Lydia Rosa: today is Tuesday and it's cold.
In your gray stone house, you sleep at the edge
Of the city. Do you still hang onto your lovesick heart
Now that you've died of love? I'll tell you what's happening:

The man you adored, the man with the cruel gray eyes,
He's smoking his cigarette in the autumn afternoon.
From behind the windowpanes, he watches the yellow sky
And the street in which faded papers swirl.

He takes a book,draws near the cold heater,
And sitting down, he turns it on.
Only the noise of clawed paper can be heard.

Five o'clock. You fell into his arms at that hour,
And maybe he remembers you...But his soft bed
Now holds the warm hollow of another rosy body.

MF and MC

THE MILKY WAY

White pollen of worlds, sweet milk of the sky,
how I wish I were a great holy butterfly
so I could plunge my head into your impalpable flour,
and drink you as if you belonged to the earth!

Now spring burns again in my eyes.
But my human passion lies, stem broken,
and the world is so lonely with my soul dried up
that I walk and my steps echo among the spheres.

And on snowy nights, when I hear the white skeletons
of the dead in spite of their stillness, the stars
moving above, it all overcomes me

as if it were a desire from the heavens, and I don't know
what I'd give to have fall on my miserable brow
one drop of Juno's milk.

MF

I AM USELESS

In order to follow the rhythm of things
Sometimes I've wanted in this active century
To think, to fight, to live with the living
And to be another gear in the world.

But tied to the seductive dream world
Of my instincts, I returned to my dark hole
Where, like a lazy and greedy insect
I was born for love.

I am useless, heavy, slow and clumsy.
My body, stretched out in the sun, feeds itself
And I only live well in the summertime

When the jungle smells and the coiled snake
Sleeps on the dry earth
And fruit drops into my hand.

JN

THE MOMENT

A city of gray bones
lies abandoned at my feet.

The piles of bones
are separated by black trenches,
the streets,
divided by them,
ordered, raised by them.
In the city, bristling with two million men,
I haven't a single one to love me.

The sky, even grayer
than the city,
descends over me,
takes over my life,
stops up my arteries,
turns off my voice...

However,
the world,
like a whirlwind
from which I can't escape,
turns round a dead point:
my heart.

MF and MC

LONELINESS

From here, I could throw my heart
over a rooftop.
My heart would roll away
without anyone seeing it.

I could shout
my pain
till my body breaks in two:
my pain would be dissolved
by the waters of the river.

I could dance
the black dance of death
over the roof:
the wind would carry
my dance away.

Setting free the blaze in my breast,
I could
send it rolling
like foolish fires:
the electric lights
would outshine them.

MC and MF

AND THE HEAD BEGAN TO BURN

On the black
wall
a square
opened up
that looked out
over the void.

And the moon rolled
up to the window;
it stopped
and said to me:
"I'm not moving from here;
I'm looking at you.

I don't want to grow
or get thin.
I'm the infinite
flower
that opens up
in the square hole
in your house.

I no longer want
to roll on
behind
the lands
that you don't know,
my butterfly,
sipper of shadows.

Or raise phantoms
over the far off
cupolas
that drink me.

I'm watching,
I see you."

And I didn't answer.
A head was sleeping
under my hands.

White,
like you,
moon.

The wells of its eyes
held a dark
water
streaked
with luminous snakes.

And suddenly
my head
began to burn
like the stars
at twilight.

And my hands
were stained
with a phosphorescent
substance.

And with it
I burn
the houses
of men,
the forests
of beasts.

MF

PROPHECY

One day
the city which I see
from above
will rise up on its flanks
and walk.
Its great iron oars
moving
in a solemn
rhythm
will advance upriver
and the water will hold them up.
With its broad blunt prow
made for piercing
into gigantic tunnels
its forests of chimneys
—black lances—
its fogs and its knots
of smoke
—waving flags—
and its army of dark
houses,
predetermined,
it will leave its humid
colonial basements
and crossing the sea
will enter
the worn out and luminous
land of
men.

MF

DRIZZLE

Colorless, icy,
the houses—
niches in a row—
huddle against
each other.

The sun
plays
in distant
gardens;
its remote steps
depress
the sky.

The smoke plumes
can't find it:
staggering since their birth,
they hug the crosses
and clutch the domes.

There was a river on the shore
of the city...
it has started walking
too,
into the sea,
with silky
feet.

Or has the misty yawn
of the afternoon
slowly swallowed it?

The chimneys
are pressed
against the horizon:
their hairpins hunt
dully
for the wings of sulky angels
who, with leaps,
brush against the cornices.

A ribbon of milky
light
binds the waist
of the city:
the fringed tips
of the lasso
lash the sky's arch
until the grains of water
soak them
and they droop.

MF

TOWER

Suspended in the air,
my house breathes in
through its wide windows,
solar energy.
The sky encloses it
in its maddening ring
and circulates through it
from one end to the other
in long, wide
rivers of light.
In its center,
my body
a sad and solitary island,
calm against the current,
takes everything in.

MF

BOATS

Over the violet plain
of the river,
three black boats
depart toward the horizon.
I can't see them move
but every minute
they get smaller.
Is the river a mallow-flower dream?
The sky a pale
blue dream?
The jungle of houses
a gold dream?
An invisible hand
pushes the boats
toward unknown
docks.
Are they going to emigrate
from the earth
in silence?
Their crests of smoke
trace signs
on the blue curtain
of the beyond.
But the air
pulls them apart,
and the words
can't be read.

MF

MEN IN THE CITY

The forests of the
horizon burn;
dodging flames,
the blue bucks
of the twilight
cross quickly.

Little gold goats
emigrate toward
the arch of the sky
and lie down
on blue moss.

Below,
there rises,
enormous,
the cement rose,
the city
unmoving on its stem
of somber basements.

Its black pistils—
dormers, towers—
emerge
to wait for lunar
pollen.

Suffocated
by the flames of bonfires,
and lost
among the petals
of the rose,
almost invisible,
moving from one side toward the other,
the men...

MF

STREET

An alley open
between high gray wallls.
At any moment: the dark mouth of the doors,
the tunnels of the entries,
traps that lead
to human catacombs.
Isn't there a shudder
in the entrance halls?
A bit of terror
in the rising whiteness
of a stairway?
I pass by hastily.
Every eye that looks at me
doubles me and scatters me
through the city.

A forest of legs,
a whirlwind
of rolling circles,
a cloud of shouts and sounds,
separate my head from my body,
my hands from my arms,
my heart from my chest,
my feet from my legs,
my will from its source.
Up above
the blue sky
calms its transparent water:
cities of gold
sail across it.

MF

EQUATION

My arms:
burst out from my shoulders;
my arms: wings.
Not feathered, but watery...
They glide over roof terraces,
they glide higher...they form a canopy.
They flow into rains;
into sea waters
and into tears,
with a human gracefulness.

My tongue:
it's ripe...
Rivers full of flowers
flow from their petals.

My heart:
abandons me.
It circulates
through invisible elliptical
circles.
It's pure blooded, heavy,
and on fire...
It grazes the valleys,
burns the peaks,
dries out the marshes...
Sunlight adds its other eye...
(and new worlds dances
all around it.)

My legs:
grow inland,
they vanish, they take hold;
they are curved tentacles
made of pressed fiber: they are oak trees
in the wind, now,
they balance my aching body.

My head: it's so light.
My eyes: forget-me-nots
which drink up the sky
and swallow wild comets,
defeated stars,
and sowed fields.

My body: it explodes.
and chains of hearts
circle my waist.
The immortal snake
coils itself around my neck.

JN

PORTRAIT OF GARCIA LORCA

Looking for the roots of wings
his forehead
moves to the right
and to the left.

Over the whirlwind of his face
a curtain of death is drawn,
thick and twisted.

A wild animal
snarls in his face
trying to destroy him
in its rage.

His distant eyes
suggest Grecian eyes...

The Andalusian hills
of his cheekbones
and the trembling valley
of his mouth
are smothered in climbing vines.

A scream
leaps from his throat
begging
for moonlit knives
made of sharp-edged water.

Slice the throat.
From north to south.
From east to west.

Let the head fly
(only the head)
wounded by dark
ocean waves.
Let the mane of the satyr
fall on him
like bell-shaped flowers
on the face
of an ancient mask.

Silence his huge voice
in its nasal passages.

Free him from it
and from his gentle arms
and earthly body.

Before throwing
his body into space
force his arched eyebrows
to become bridges
of the Atlantic
and Pacific

So that his eyes
like lost ships
can sail,
without ports
or shores.

JN

CITY JUNGLE

In a semi-circle
the jungle of houses
opens:
some beside each other,
some behind each other,
some above each other,
some in front of each other,
all remote from each other.
They are gray masses that get along well
until their branches dry up
in the cold southern air.
Gray masses which multiply
until smoke from northern ovens
loosens their joints.
Always cross-hatched,
they repeat themselves by angles
with the same toy shop windows,
the same flat red roofs,
the same brown towers,
the same faded entrances,
the same dark gratings,
the same red mailboxes,
the same black columns,
the same yellow lights.
Underneath the roofs
another jungle,
a human jungle
must move;
but not in a straight line.
Strange tree trunks
with luminous tops
sway visibly
moved by a wind
which does not speak.
But I don't understand their shapes
nor hear their words
nor see the splendor
of their eyes.
The walls are very thick,
the roofs very heavy.

JN

LIGHTHOUSE AT NIGHT

The sky is a black sphere
and the sea is a black disc.

On the coast the lighthouse unfolds
its fan of light.

Who is it looking for endlessly in the night
as it turns endlessly?

If it looks into my breast
it will find a dying heart.

Look at the black rock
where my heart is nailed.

A raven tears at it without stopping
but it no longer bleeds.

JN

TO EROS

I caught you by the neck
on the shore of the sea, while you shot
arrows from your quiver to wound me
and on the ground I saw your flowered crown.

I disemboweled your stomach like a doll's
and examined your deceitful wheels,
and deeply hidden in your golden pulleys
I found a trapdoor that said: sex.

On the beach I held you, now a sad heap,
up to the sun, accomplice of your deeds,
before a chorus of frightened sirens.

Your deceitful godmother, the moon
was climbing through the crest of the dawn,
and I threw you into the mouth of the waves.

KS

TO MY LADY OF POETRY

I throw myself here at your feet, sinful,
my dark face against your blue earth,
you the virgin among armies of palm trees
that never grow old as humans do.

I don't dare look at your pure eyes
or dare touch your miraculous hand:
I look behind me and a river of rashness
urges me guiltlessly on against you.

With a promise to mend my ways through your
divine grace, I humbly place on your
hem a little green branch,

for I couldn't have possibly lived
cut off from your shadow, since you blinded me
at birth with your fierce branding iron.

KS

42

A HEN

An ordinary afternoon. Under the water
the voices of every dead thing,
and the sun stamps on the day a lovely ex-libris
in gold, cobalt blue, and bright pink.

My mind isn't creative enough to lay
seige to life. It flies to the country,
escaping the trap of the distracted eye.
Why do I notice the obscure hen

going down to the beach, at her sides
her two wind-whipped bustles?
Why do I follow her lonely tracks

that mark out lilies in the golden dust?
Will this sand, dredged up from the seas,
keep her innocent prints for fossils?

MF

RETURN TO MY BIRDS

I didn't listen to your frugal concert,
my birds, for I saw a city of mirrors with gold
battlements and under its streetlights
not hands beckoning, but flags.

And from its lofty patrol great voices
of pompous acoustics; and I held my finger close
and the cardboard city fell
and the livid air wrote: misery.

Now I'm once more in your hearts, alone,
and the stars' orbital technique
isn't better than yours, precious flight.

Now I listen once more, unfettered,
and you, my little one, how you sing
on my balcony: 'Why hast thou forsaken me?'

MF

SUPERTELEPHONE

"Can I speak to Horatio?" I know that now
you have a nest of doves in your bladder,
and you crystal motorcycle flies
silently through the air.

"Papa?" I dreamed that your flask
swelled up like the Tupungato River;
it still holds your anger and my poems.
Pour me a drop. Thanks. Now I feel fine.

I'll be seeing you both very soon. Come to meet me
with that frog I killed at our country house
in San Juan; poor frog—we stoned it to death.

It looked at us like an ox, and my two cousins
finished it off; later it had a funeral
with skillets banging, and roses followed it.

MF

DEPARTURE

A road
to the limit:
high golden doors
close it off;
deep galleries;
arcades...

The air has no weight;
the doors stand by themselves
in the emptiness;
they disintegrate into golden dust;
they close, they open;
they go down to the algae
tombs;
they come up loaded with coral.

Patrols,
there are patrols of coluumns;
the doors hide
behind the blue parapets;
water bursts into fields of forget-me-nots;
it tosses up deserts of purple crystals;
it incubates great emerald worms;
it plaits its innumerable arms.

A rain of wings,
now;
pink angels
dive like arrows
into the sea.
I could walk on them
without sinking.
A path of ciphers
for my feet;
columns of numbers
for each step—
submarine.

They carry me:
invisible vines
stretch out their hooks
from the horizon.
My neck creaks.
I walk.
The water holds its own.
My shoulders open into wings.
I touch the ends of the sky
with their tips.
I wound it.
The sky's blood
bathing the sea...
poppies, poppies,
there is nothing but poppies.

I grow light:
the flesh falls from my bones.
Now.
The sea rises through the channels
of my spine.
Now.
The sky rolls through the bed
of my veins.
Now.
The sun! The sun!
Its last rays
envelop me,
push me:
I am a spindle
I spin, spin, spin, spin!

MF

FISHERMEN

At the edge of the water
the yellow poles
offer death ties.

The sun sleeps without anger
on the hand
which patiently waits.

Finally,
a tiny fish
tinges with blue
the tip of the hook.

And a piece of the sky,
smaller than a rose petal,
flops on the ground,
wounded to death.

Useless drama:
the fisherman once again dips
his rod,
and the sun, without anger,
once again sleeps on his hand.

MF

TO A ROSE

Grateful flower, you stand out
above the green of your leaves,
like the blood of a wound,
           Red...Red...

You parody those purple lips
which, half-open,
could be called kisses
of thirsty people.

The leading champions of your ideas
have copied the color
of your leaves
for their flag.

And that's why I worship you,
beautiful flower, because above the leaves' green
you stand out
           Red...Red...

MF

HE PASSED BY

It was at night...My spirit
trembled from sadness...
The windows creaked. Snow... snow on the branches...

It was at night; my life was a total black night;
my life was a stream bed collecting frost,
and they said to me: Look,
he's going to pass by your house!

And I looked at him! He was carrying
in his dark hands a handful of dawns:
In his eyes, seeds of the truth. His soles
were made of sun because they shed light,
and doves, lord, his words were doves.

And I opened the doors of my house wide
and I opened my heart,
like a window.
Sun enters through windows, and at that hour
sun's white doves entered my heart.

He went on his way
without looking into my eyes; without looking into my soul.
He went on his way....
His grace wasn't for me!

My house and its windows
           Are closed again
closed.
           The night has returned: Snow
falls, and snow on the branches.

MF

TRAIN

The train leaves: I dream,
leaning
on a windowsill.

Nothing:
Rails, plants, thresher,
the smiling landscape,
not one of them tempts me to look.

The train traces a curve
and I put out my head:
way back there the smudged vision
of the city I left disturbs me,
staining my sadness.

I'm leaving my love...The train
moves slowly.
Someone shouts my name. Who is it?
I let my forehead fall
onto my forearm and I say:
Hurry on, train, be fierce,
and finish me off.

MF

CLOUDS AND SAILS

Neck stretched out,
wings in the form of a cross,
beak gasping,
a monstrous heron
comes from the river:
the tips of its pink wings
stretch out to the river's edges,
its neck, golden down,
throws off black rays
over the violet steel
of the water.
Its beak, a mother-of-pearl knife,
reaches out to thread together
the black
 bridges of the river's mouth.
Under awnings
of illusion,
the sailboats,
huge white butterflies,
giddily snap
at the flat plate
of the river.

MF

FOG

Heavy plants of fog
spring from the earth;
they rise up clinging to the walls
and strangle them.
They weave their branches
from wall to wall
and drape the city.
Occasionally
a sharp prow
scatters the jungle of humidity,
pulls it apart,
and breathes.
Bold branches want to climb
high as roofs,
but they weigh too much
and fall in bunches
over the roofs.
Bells and car horns
sound a hoarse
noise of alarm,
down below,
in the invisible depths
where dim monsters
dizzingly change
places on the asphalt.
Do warning bells
ring like that
at the ocean's bottom?
Meanwhile the lit up street,
a long many-colored
snake,
puts down its head and tail
at opposite ends
and pushing its glittering
back upward
overcomes the gray withered leaves
and sparkles.

MF

DROP

Oh little goldfinch,
Speak of your happiness,
It's summer, it's June,
The fruit is heavenly.

What does my luck matter to you?
I am here speechless,
Knowing what death is,
But you know nothing.

Fly, for children are playing
In the Meadow,
The vine is growning
And the world goes on turning...

MF

TO NORAH LANGE
(WHO WROTE A BOOK: THE ROUTE OF THE ROSE)

Where will your rose drop anchor,
Norah?

You threw it out to wander
through the green channels
of the soul,
over waves of silence;

in the round
afternoons, of Buenos Aires perfumes:

beyond the sphere
of yourself.

At times it balanced itself
over the nothingness of a lagoon
in an ecstasy of peace.

Or stretched out like a worm
to slip between
the straits
of anguish.

Or attached itself
on the highest point
of a cliff:
a bird of fire.

It wasn't always
a rose...

Now it would crawl
up the black
chimney of the city,
a painter rat
checking out landscapes.

Or it was a huntress
of children's heads,
flowers of fleeing feet...

Or it donned two paper
wings:
a sad letter,
a tiny airplane
cutting through mists...

It could cause pain
like the root
of an ancient tree.

Or it was a mill
of a flowery heart,
the white of rock salt,
a percolator of uncolored
petals.

It knew how to reduce the world
to the size
of a window's square.

A double jawbone of twenty-four hours,
one morning lip,
the other nocturnal,
it imprisoned a yawn
which was solitude.

And it called to the birds
of silence
to hatch
in your mouth
the kiss that doesn't wound.

Route of the Rose,
sailing through the water of books
Where no limits are possible...!

What new Atlantis
will hunt you
through such a vast ocean?

MF

NIGHT

Thanks, night:
not because the moon returns
or the stars live
or the crickets sing
in the damp marble.

Thanks because you dissolve
the dirtiness of the streets
with your invisible veils.

MF

DOG AND SEA

The sea was alone
and the sky alone
and everything was gray
and cold space
and I heard nothing,
saw nothing
more than that monotonous
and lifeless gray.

And at my side
the dog howled against the wind,
and his barking
shook the dead waves;
and his grumbling
broke open a path
in the lead air;
and his tense ears
seemed to rise up like antennas
toward dismantled throats.

Were there nests
of live mice
where my dry eyes
couldn't see?

Ghosts nestling
in the far off
peaks
of the waters?

And did underground
forces appear
on the wall
of the wind?

And was someone
dressing the sea
and streaking it
with multicolored parks,
there on the bottom
across its face of shadows?

This time
and endless howl
stood up
from the sea's lifted head
and the head took off running
toward the town,
fleeing the sea
as if someone
had ordered it to leave.

And my heart,
crazy for no reason,
feeling abandoned,
set in flight
a bell of twilight.

MF

HEAD AND SEA

On the beach,
a dark point,
a head.
Lying there.

Two seagull wings
could cover
the sad skull
in the clamped
pincers
of the sky.

From the head
spiderwebs
are born and expand,
they go hunting
among invisible threads
to the sounds
of intimate voices of the sea;
and they bring down lives
from the high glass;
and they trap
far off forests
that undulate
beyond the sea.

The head
in its interior
spaces moves
impalpable pulleys,
and there is neither shadow nor light
which the sea reflects
that is not tied
inside to the finest
of its numerical
wheels.

Now the raised
head looks at
the great plains
of water
which threaten
to throw themselves over it
and destroy it;
but they only die
on the cold
beach.
The focus of its eyes
exchange
blue sparks
with the sea force,
and the eye
cuts the sea
and runs it through
with a long
thrust
which brings blood
of eternal
algae.

MF

TOAD AND SEA

Lead blue,
the sea
wove yellow
dawns about it.

And a toad
dropped
the metallic
splash of its speech
over the sea's dusky voice.

The infinite open
on my right;
on my left
the farthest point
was breaking
in a green
of rusted
moss.

Alone. Scattered.
A frozen
curtain
tolled the yes...no...
of fleeting
thought.

And a cup of tea
in front of my eyes
was the only line
that tied me—
sad animal—
to the mortal chain.

MF

TROPIC

White stone,
the burning sky
falls over the dry
land.

The forests burn
in red rings
and the curtains of smoke
swallow landscapes
and towns dry up.

Held in their beds,
the waters
make coins
of their blank surfaces.

Devils, their wings on fire,
crisscross the fields
in a whirling dance.

Along the limestone
embankments
the glowing embers of the train
cross shrieking.

Dragged
by the hellish white,
the seed-laden sole of my foot,
returned home,
now is going to grow
jungle roots,
not human ones.

And from my breast
no milky sap
is going to sprout:
instead, the mountains'
sharp stone.

MF

MARY CROW is a poet and translator who teaches at Colorado State University in the Department of English. In 1979 she won the Columbia University Translation Award for her book of translations of Spanish-American women poets, *Woman who has sprouted wings*. She has traveled extensively in Latin America on various grants studying and translating surrealist poetry. She has recently been a Fulbright poet in Yugoslavia. Her poetry has appeared in numerous journals and in two chapbooks.

MARION FREEMAN teaches Spanish at Colorado State University. She has read and published literary studies in medieval and Renaissance literature as well as on twentieth century Spanish and Spanish-American authors. Her work includes feminist criticism, and her translations of poetry by Spanish-American women poets have appeared in magazines and anthologies.

JIM NORMINGTON is a poet and a translator from the Spanish. His poems and translations have appeared in journals in the United States, Canada, and Japan. He is the author of seven books of poetry, the most recent being *Radioactive Knives.* He has translated the *Selected Poems* of Efrain Huerta of Mexico and also *The Elemental Odes* of Pablo Neruda. He teaches English as a Second Language in Sacramento, California.

KAY SHORT is a graduate student in English at Colorado State University. As an undergraduate, she wrote an honors thesis on Alfonsina Storni which included translations and a feminist analysis of her love poems.

Printed in the USA
CPSIA information can be obtained
at www.ICGtesting.com
JSHW082224140824
68134JS00015B/733